BANDS

Paul A. Rabbitts

SHIRE PUBLICATIONS

Published in Great Britain in 2011 by Shire Publications Ltd, Midland House, West Way, Botley, Oxford OX2 0PH, United Kingdom.

44-02 23rd Street, Suite 219, Long Island City, NY 11101, USA.

E-mail: shire@shirebooks.co.uk   www.shirebooks.co.uk

A CIP catalogue record for this book is available from the British Library.

Shire Library no. 625.   ISBN-13: 978 0 74780 825 1

Paul A. Rabbitts has asserted his right under the Copyright, Designs and Patents Act, 1988, to be identified as the author of this book.

Designed by Tony Truscott Designs, Sussex, UK and typeset in Perpetua and Gill Sans.

Printed in China through Worldprint Ltd.

11 12 13 14 15   10 9 8 7 6 5 4 3 2 1

COVER IMAGE
The bandstand at Brighton. Photograph by kind permission of Andrew Levey, www.andrewlevey.co.uk

TITLE PAGE IMAGE
Leazes Park, Newcastle upon Tyne: the Sun Foundry bandstand, erected in 1875 at a cost of £155 10s, was dismantled in 1940, but replaced in 2003. Despite the difference in design, the baluster panels are identical to those in Lincoln Arboretum.

CONTENTS PAGE IMAGE
St Annes-on-Sea, Lancashire Lion Foundry bandstand.

DEDICATION
This book is dedicated to my family, Julie, Ashley, Holly and Ellie Rabbitts.

ACKNOWLEDGEMENTS
My thanks go to the following: David Lambert and Stewart Harding at the Parks Agency; Maurice Bradbury, a fellow bandstand enthusiast; the Scottish Ironwork Foundation; colleagues from Halcrow who live and work all over the country and have provided many images, locations and local histories; the many local authorities who continue to send me information on their own bandstands; and, finally, my family for putting up with me while I stand gazing most weekends at another Walter MacFarlane model 279.

Illustrations are acknowledged as follows:

Marina Argyrou, page 59; Blackburn with Darwen Library and Information Services, page 15; David Coke, pages 5 and 10; Centre for Local Studies at Darlington Library, page 46; Dorman Museum, Middlesbrough (Middlesbrough Council), page 54; East Dunbartonshire Council (licensor www.scran.ac.uk), pages 31, 33, 34, 60 and 62; Edinburgh City Council, page 48; University of Glasgow (licensor www.scran.ac.uk), page 8; Jennie Peacock, page 56; Perth Museum & Art Gallery (licensor www.scran.ac.uk), page 6; Rotherham Archives & Local Studies Service, page 57; The Scotsman Publications Ltd, pages 44, 46, 48; Scottish Ironwork Foundation, page 19; Tameside Council, pages 32, 42, 58; Walsall Local History Centre, page 21 (top); Amy-Louise Webber, page 51.

All other images belong to the author.

Shire Publications is supporting the Woodland Trust, the UK's leading woodland conservation charity, by funding the dedication of trees.

CONTENTS

INTRODUCTION

IN JULY 1937 the music critic Jack Donaldson wrote in the *Daily Express* column 'Music Notes': 'If you are fond of music, of the open air and of your fellow Londoners, why not go to the parks for your music?' He goes on to describe Myatt's Fields, Camberwell, London, as

> a pretty little park which not long ago was a market garden, with cabbages growing instead of flowers, as I was informed. The band plays in a circular railed bandstand, with a wider circle of railings shutting off a space from the tennis and cricket. I arrived punctually at 7.30, but there was no sign of room on the seats and I couldn't squeeze onto the railings. So I selected a tree to lean against, which I shared with a thin elderly workman.

The scene described would have been typical of most parks across the United Kingdom. To relax on the grass in a park, with the local brass band seated on a picturesque bandstand and preparing to strike up an air, was the quintessence of summer bliss from the 1860s to the end of the Second World War.

By the end of the nineteenth century bandstands were so popular that no town park or seaside promenade was considered complete without one. From St Andrews in Scotland to Penzance in Cornwall, through the industrial heartlands of the Midlands, Yorkshire and Lancashire, and the Victorian splendour of Britain's coastal resorts, bandstands served as symbols of local identity, civic pride and a community's cultural commitment.

Bandstands became the focal points of parks and seaside promenades – colourful, elegant structures, often made of cast iron and ornately decorated, or else constructed of timber or concrete and thus more often simplistic in design. Park users and seaside visitors have always loved these structures and during their decline in the second half of the twentieth century their dereliction became symptomatic of the decline of public parks in particular, but also of many seaside resorts.

Their origins lie in the design of the great pleasure gardens which, with their winning formula of combined music, illuminated fountains, fireworks and light refreshments in an Eden-like atmosphere, preceded the monumental parks movement of the Victorian era. Bandstands were originally designed as focal points within grand designs, as shelters, viewing points and belvederes, and ultimately as a focus for musical pleasure. Originally simplistic, they were inexpensive: Frederick Law Olmsted and Calvert Vaux included only $5,000 for 'music platforms, arbors and seats' out of the $1,500,000 construction budget for Central Park in New York in 1872.

Who pioneered the introduction of these bandstands and paid for them? Local councils were the main instigators, as well as a number of local benefactors, philanthropists and charities, buying 'off the shelf' bandstands designed by a few foundries which had cornered the market but also designed a number of bespoke bandstands. The bandstand in Lincoln Arboretum was erected on the large lawn in front of the terrace in 1884 at a cost of £120 and was sponsored by the Lincoln Lodges of Oddfellows. At a ceremony in front of ten thousand people the Mayor pronounced:

> I think the brass band concerts are a great improvement on the so called fetes that have been held in years past. There cannot, in my opinion, be a more sickening sight than to witness three or four painted brazen images in tights, dancing about on a raised platform in the broad light of heaven.

The bandstand was restored in 2002 as part of the park's refurbishment.

Today, bandstands evoke sentimental memories of simpler days when music had the power to bridge social and cultural barriers. Compared to the period before the Second World War, when they were at their peak, few remain today. From old postcards and local archives, as well as from the few restoration specialists, however, one quickly discovers the stunning diversity of the architecture of bandstands and of their role in the urban fabric, in particular that of public parks and seaside resorts.

An engraving called 'A Perspective View of Vaux Hall Garden' by J. Maurer of 1744, which shows the original (1735) orchestra stand. Canaletto also painted a view of the Grand Walk in 1751. The *Gentleman's Magazine* reported on 21 April 1749: '... was performed at Vauxhall Gardens the rehearsal of the music [Handel's *Music for the Royal Fireworks*] by a band of 100 musicians, to an audience above 12,000 persons (tickets 2s 6d).'

BANDSTANDS IN PARKS

THE ORIGIN and history of bandstands in parks are linked with the evolution and decline of public parks in our society and their subsequent revival in the twenty-first century.

During the mid-nineteenth century urban parks were created throughout Britain as a response to the appalling problems of the urban environment brought about by industrialisation and rapid population growth. Britain was at the forefront of the Industrial Revolution and was the first country to develop the municipal park. Official recognition of the need for parks dates from 1833, when the Select Committee on Public Walks presented a report to Parliament about the open space available for recreation in major industrial centres and smaller towns. The Committee concluded that the poorest people living in the largest urban centres in overcrowded conditions of utmost poverty had the greatest need for parks. Only London, with its Royal Parks, had an adequate provision of parks, but even in the capital there were no parks in the East End or south of the river, except for Greenwich Park. The urban park was to be seen as simulated countryside. There were economic as well as social reasons for providing parks. Recreation and exercise in the open air would improve physical fitness. This would increase productivity and prolong the economically active life of city and town dwellers. There were also moral motives. The Committee was convinced that 'some open spaces reserved for the amusement of the humbler classes would assist to wean them from low and debasing pleasures'.

The parks movement began slowly in the 1830s and 1840s, when parks began to be created in the major industrial towns of the north-west of England and in Glasgow. The first of the new industrial centres to create a municipal park was Preston, Lancashire, where Moor Park opened in 1833, closely followed by Manchester, with Philips Park and Queens's Park, and Salford with Peel Park. Glasgow created its first park, Kelvingrove Park, in 1854. As the park movement expanded, benefactors and philanthropists donated parks, but by far the greatest number were created by local authorities, for whom their parks were a cause for great civic pride.

Opposite:
The bandstand on the North Inch, Perth, about 1903.

Middlesbrough in north-east England, established in 1830, soon became an important centre of heavy industry, including ironworks, shipbuilding and railways, accompanied by industrial pollution. In 1859 the council was already considering its first public park and the *Middlesbrough Advertiser* in October 1859 reported on the subject of a people's park for the town.

Glasgow's first area of common land was Glasgow Green in the heart of the city, next to the River Clyde. However, in the nineteenth century some far-sighted town planners, seeing that the city was expanding rapidly, bought several large areas of land to be made into public parks. Kelvingrove, in the west of the city, was the first of these. Bandstands were erected there for the 1901 and 1911 Exhibitions.

We are sure that if inhabitants of the town were appealed to in the matter, they would liberally come forward in its support. The want is felt by all classes in the town. No place is so badly provided for the recreative department as ours. Sickly looking youth and pallid manhood would receive a boon indeed by the establishment of some recreative institution or the enclosure of some ground where cramped limbs might be exercised, and the mind be dragged from the everlasting monotony around us. The lobes of the lungs are nowhere so severely tested as here and it is paramount opinion everywhere that we live in the smokiest, unhealthiest hole in the kingdom.

It was not until 1865, however, that land was bequeathed to the inhabitants of Middlesbrough by a local benefactor, Henry William Ferdinand Bolckow, who decreed that

the Park should be called Albert Park, the extent of land to be devoted to the Park to be about seventy one acres, that the sum of £3,000 should be expended in laying out the Park under the direction of the donor, that the Council should apply to Parliament for an Act, that not less than £500 be spent annually in maintaining the park, that no intoxicating drinks be allowed to be sold within its precincts.

Lister Park, Bradford, was laid out between 1870 and 1904 on the site of the gardens and park of Manningham Hall. The bandstand was built in 1908, at a cost of £644. In its first year, over £600 was spent on bands alone. Terracing, long since gone, which overlooked the bandstand, used to be packed with people listening to bands.

Many parks were created during this pioneering phase between 1830 and 1885, but many more were created between 1885 and 1914 to meet the growing need, first voiced by the Parliamentary Committee in stressing that parks would improve people's physical health, make them happier and better citizens, and encourage them to be virtuous.

Light and airy, painted in bold colours and set against a background of green, the bandstand came to symbolise the public park. The introduction of a bandstand brought new life and soul to many early Victorian parks. In 1884, around ten thousand visitors attended the installation of the new bandstand in Lincoln Arboretum, with a host of concerts and contests following. Some of these contests caused great controversy: in 1887, for instance, the judge's decision aroused such animosity that the police had to protect him from being mobbed until he was able to escape to the railway station in a cab. However, it was also the disappearance or dereliction of the bandstand that was one of the clearest indicators of the decline of the public park, when local authorities were unwilling or unable to repair, restore or replace these iconic structures.

So how did bandstands evolve and why does the history of their introduction, flourishing and decline so closely reflect the popularity of the public park? In 1873 Victoria Park in London was described as the best people's park in the city because of the facilities it offered. The *Illustrated London News* published a whole page of views, including the Chinese Pagoda, a bridge, a boathouse and a refreshment saloon. Victoria Park was clearly a popular place to go because of the facilities available, and it was the design of the parks and the facilities they provided that ensured that they have remained popular, despite their subsequent decline.

The inspiration for the design and creation of many public parks and the buildings within them, such as lodges, shelters, boathouses, band houses, pagodas, monuments and sculptures, came from the private parks and pleasure gardens of the eighteenth century. Palm houses and winter gardens were developed in the early years of the nineteenth century before public parks came into being and were found on many grand estates throughout Britain. Refreshment rooms and the early forms of the bandstand had their precursors in public pleasure gardens such as Vauxhall Gardens, London and the Larmer Tree Gardens near Salisbury, Wiltshire. Created by General Pitt Rivers in 1880 as pleasure grounds for 'public enlightenment and entertainment', the Larmer Tree Gardens are an extraordinary example of Victorian extravagance and vision. On inheriting the Rushmore Estate, General Pitt Rivers almost immediately set about creating these pleasure grounds, which by 1899 were attracting over 44,000 visitors a year. Around the main lawn he constructed a variety of buildings intended to enlighten and educate estate workers and visitors. For visitors wishing to picnic, there were eight areas, known as 'quarters', each enclosed by laurel hedges and containing a thatched building for shelter. Music and entertainment were closely associated with the gardens. The Singing Theatre was used for plays and poetry recitals, and in a field adjoining the gardens were a racecourse, lawn tennis courts and an eighteen-hole

The second orchestra stand at Vauxhall was built in 1757 and lasted, in various forms, until the final closure in 1859.

golf course. In the evening the gardens were illuminated with thousands of Vauxhall lights, and there was dancing in the open air. Thomas Hardy described it in 1895 as 'quite the prettiest sight I ever saw in my life'.

In the United States bandstands developed in much the same way as in the United Kingdom. They were perceived purely as functional pieces of civic architecture, often placed within public squares. However, a fresh current in landscape architecture caused Americans increasingly to view bandstands and similar structures as vital links between people and nature. The new sensibility dictated that the bandstand fit picturesquely into a pastoral landscape. The bucolic conception of the bandstand had been set out by landscape architect Andrew Jackson Downing in *A Treatise on the Theory and Practice of Landscape Gardening*: 'There is scarcely a prettier or more pleasant object for the termination of a long walk in the pleasure grounds or park than a neatly thatched structure of rustic work.' The gazebos he contrived to fill this function were prototypes for a new form of bandstand.

A gazebo, from *A Treatise on the Theory and Practice of Landscape Gardening* by A. J. Downing.

It was, however, Frederick Law Olmsted, architect of New York City's Central Park, who drew the link between such sylvan bowers and music: 'The effect of good music on the Park is to aid the mind in freeing itself from the irritating effect of the urban conditions.' In other words, the modern city should contain its own antidote in the form of rural parks, which should be sprinkled with garden houses, gazebos, pavilions and 'concert groves', where weary urbanites would be soothed by pleasing tunes.

As with the movement in park design in the United Kingdom, Americans of the late nineteenth century were concluding that parks and band music were needed to humanise the growing industrial city. Their resulting bandstands were designed to serve as settings for informal concerts and, at other times, as belvederes from which walkers could view their pleasant surroundings. To enhance their function as belvederes, bandstands were elevated further from the ground. The belvedere and the bandstand were in some cases difficult to distinguish.

In his early planning for Central Park, Frederick Law Olmsted cautioned against 'grandiose architectural display' that would distract from one's appreciation of nature. By 1880, however, Olmsted's restraint was out of fashion. Even his former partner, Calvert Vaux, was creating more elaborate bandstands, and in city after city architects and builders competed to achieve ever more extravagant displays of virtuosity. More modest bandstands continued to be built, but they were no longer the rule. The availability of inexpensive millwork and factory-made turnings, such as columns and balustrades, as well as polychrome tiles and cast-iron columns and handrails,

Acton Recreation Ground, Middlesex, laid out in 1888, at a cost of £26,300, to benefit the parish of Acton, and opened in 1889 with the Acton Town Band and Hanwell District schools bands playing. The Acton Town Band played at the bandstand on Wednesday afternoons, when the shops closed at lunchtime, and, by 1903, on Sundays too. The simply designed bandstand was rebuilt in 1911.

The elegant Peckham Rye bandstand was one of the original bandstands designed by Captain Francis Fowke and made for the Royal Horticultural Society stand at the International Exhibition in South Kensington in 1862, after which it was sold to the London County Council (LCC). Re-erected in Peckham Rye in south-east London, it was formally opened on 13 July 1889 but was destroyed during the Second World War.

was an irresistible temptation both to big cities and to small towns. Bandstands thus took on yet another function – to serve as bright and whimsical pieces of urban sculpture.

By the end of the nineteenth century bandstands had become so popular that no park was considered complete without one. In the United Kingdom the first bandstands, or 'band houses' as they were also called, were built in the Royal Horticultural Society Gardens, South Kensington, which opened in 1861. These bandstands were designed by Captain Francis Fowke of the Royal Engineers, the architect of the main quadrangle of the Victoria and Albert Museum and of the Royal Albert Hall. They were circular domed pavilions supported by slender cast-iron columns. A similar pavilion was displayed at the Paris Industrial Exhibition, which opened in May 1855, and Fowke may well have seen it there when he was working in Paris. The form is similar to that of the *chatri*, a domed and pillared pavilion that is a feature

of many Indian and Islamic buildings. When the gardens closed, the bandstands were bought by the London County Council (LCC), which re-erected them in Southwark Park and Peckham Rye, but both were destroyed in the Second World War. The contractor who was shifting the South Kensington bandstands suggested to the council that a copy might be made for Clapham Common. The LCC architect Thomas Blashill drew up plans for a replica, slightly modified for reasons of cost. The ironwork came from George Smith's Sun Foundry in Glasgow, one of the best manufacturers of ornamental ironwork in Victorian Britain. In 1890, the Clapham Common bandstand was delivered for the sum of £598.

Clapham Common, London. Fowke's cast-iron bandstands were light and airy in design, with a wooden dome covered in zinc. The materials and the sources of the design were different from those of their predecessors, such as that at Vauxhall Gardens.

Music had been played in parks before bandstands were introduced, but bandstands provided a focus and they quickly became very popular. People either sat on seats or deckchairs to listen, or strolled around. Unlike bandstands in pleasure gardens, those in public parks were rarely the focus for dancing until later in the twentieth century. Concerts by military and works bands were the mainstay of the entertainment, often held on weekday evenings and Sundays in the summer, and they were enormously popular, but at first the playing of music on Sundays was opposed by such groups as the Sabbatarians and the Lord's Day Observance Society. Ironically, many bandstands were also used for open-air church services.

On Clapham Common, concerts were at first held only on Wednesday afternoons, but in 1891 Sunday concerts began, on condition that there was to be no dance music. The next twenty years were a great period for band concerts on the Common. Professional bands were performing, as well as the traditional police and military bands. At first, some of the seating around the bandstand was free, but from 1895 all was charged for. In 1905 the head of LCC parks wrote that Clapham was 'one of the most frequented of all the commons ... a horse ride and a bandstand make the attractions complete'.

When eleven brass bands gathered on the upper terrace of Corporation Park, Blackburn, Lancashire, in 1861, more than fifty thousand people assembled to listen, and in 1909 the *Blackburn Times* reported:

> Over 6,000 people assembled in the Blackburn Corporation Park yesterday afternoon, when the new bandstand was formally opened by Councillor J. H. Higginson, vice chairman of the Parks Committee and chairman of the Elementary Education Sub-Committee. The seating accommodation was taxed to its utmost capacity and there were hundreds of people standing round the railings ... The stand was occupied by the band of the Border Regiment ... The bandstand was then formally declared open. Blackburn can now boast one of the most up-to-date, as well as one of the prettiest, bandstand arrangements in the country. The cost of the new stand in the Corporation Park and the entire alterations is, in round figures, £2,000. Acoustic considerations have received primary attention, and the foundation of the structure occupies a lower level than the auditorium ... The bandstand itself is octagonal in shape, and has been constructed of ornamental ironwork

Cringle Fields Park, Manchester. In its early years (c. 1929) the bandstand enclosure was used for worship by the congregations of local churches. Each sector of the seating was reserved for a named church.

by The Lion Foundry Company Ltd, of Glasgow, the painting having been attractively carried out by Mr Wilkinson, of Blackburn, in a variety of light colours suited to the design. The structure, which will comfortably accommodate 60 performers ... The Music was played by the band of the 2nd Battalion of the Border Regiment, conducted by Mr W. G. Taylor. The operatic pieces in particular proved to the popular taste and altogether the audiences were very favourably impressed by the arrangements for hearing the music to the best advantage.

The bandstand was seen by many philanthropists of the time as another aspect of the reforming potential of parks. Jack Donaldson wrote in his *Daily Express* column in July 1937:

> The L.C.C. are not only concerned with refuse collection, sanitary inspection and welfare clinics. They have their human and aesthetic side and the music and entertainment they provide in the London Parks deserve a music critic's notice ... Sixty bands are engaged and play in different parks throughout the summer. Nearly every park has a band on Sunday evenings from 7 to 9 ... the acoustics of the covered bandstand are remarkable. You can hear every note from 300 yards away without difficulty.

Substantial crowds would gather for these concerts. Bandstands were not only venues for musical extravaganzas, but also for major public events,

Corporation Park, Blackburn, Lancashire. The Lion Foundry bandstand, with its amphitheatre design common in many parks at the time, was removed in 1941 for salvage for the war effort.

Queen's Park bandstand in Loughborough, Leicestershire, manufactured by Hill & Smith, and opened in 1902. Councillor Wootton proclaimed during his speech that it had often occurred to him, when he had seen young people about the streets after the shops were closed, that it would be a good thing if they had an opportunity of listening to 'a bit of good music' – which included Wagner, Strauss, Sullivan and Rossini.

public holidays and local festivals. They became focal points for many local communities.

However, bandstand designs were changing and a much wider range of bandstands was appearing in public parks, produced by a number of manufacturers, such as Walter MacFarlane of Glasgow, who published catalogues illustrating the various types that were available. These

Crowds gathering in Albert Park, Middlesbrough, around the George Smith Sun Foundry bandstand, for the 1935 Jubilee service.

Roker Park bandstand, Sunderland, erected in 1880.

manufacturers are discussed in a later chapter. MacFarlane bandstands appeared across the United Kingdom in many public parks and became extremely popular.

As well as the standard designs available from MacFarlane and other makers, the foundries also designed and erected many bespoke bandstands, most of which have now, sadly, disappeared.

Below: The Walter MacFarlane bandstand in the Spa Gardens, Ripon, North Yorkshire, was opened by the Mayor in June 1902, and the first concert was performed by the 1st Battalion, The West Yorkshire Regiment.

Wilton Lodge Park, Hawick, Scottish Borders. The bandstand was erected in 1890 by the Elmbank Foundry of Glasgow, but only the plinth now remains. The date of removal is unknown.

Left: Beveridge Park, Kirkcaldy, Fife. The park dates from 1892, when Provost Michael Beveridge bequeathed 104 acres of the Raith Estate to the people of Kirkcaldy.

Victoria Park, Haslingden, Lancashire, was presented by John Stott, a local industrialist, and opened by the Mayor in June 1901.

Rustic bandstands constructed of wood, and with a delightful simplicity of design, also became very popular, as did those built of stone. Bandstands continued to be built in parks between the wars, when concrete was the fashionable new material and was extensively used.

A small number of bandstands were designed and built in a much more unusual 'open stage' amphitheatre style. Fine examples were at Kelvingrove Park, Glasgow, built in 1924–5 by architect James Miller, at Walton Hall Park, Liverpool and a Walter MacFarlane model in Walsall Arboretum in the West Midlands.

The bandstand in Chalkwell Park or Pier Hill, Southend-on-Sea, Essex, was erected in 1896 by Walter MacFarlane's Saracen Foundry.

Rock Park, Barnstaple, Devon, was given to the town in 1879 by William Frederick Rock. Rustic in style with a thatched roof, the bandstand is simple but effective.

As bandstand styles changed, so did the activities undertaken within parks. In the period before the First World War the desire for fresh air, improved physical health and reduced mortality rates was reinforced by concern for the health of young people and the consequent need for facilities for active recreation. As a result, the National Playing Fields Association was established, and the ongoing momentum of park development was maintained between the two world wars. Indeed, Glasgow acquired half of its parks after 1925.

After the Second World War, however, times and tastes changed almost immediately. Sport came to dominate activity within public open spaces, which became playing fields or playgrounds rather than more formal parks. Cinema, radio and television provided alternative means of entertainment.

Blake Gardens, Bridgwater, Somerset. The bandstand was opened by Mrs Wills, the Mayoress, on 29 July 1908. The town had been waiting twenty years for a site for it.

A British Legion service at Walsall Arboretum, West Midlands, in September 1933. The first bandstand opened here in 1873, but this was replaced in 1924 by the shell bandstand that stands in the park today. It was built by Walter MacFarlane & Company of the Saracen Foundry, Glasgow, at a cost of £1,550.

As a result, very quickly, no more bandstands were built and those that remained fell into disuse and became empty shells. The outlook for parks and their bandstands was bleak.

Blyth beach bandstand, Northumberland, forms part of Blyth Battery, originally a gun battery used in both world wars, which in peacetime became a leisure facility, to which Blyth Links were added in the 1920s and 1930s along with the bandstand. By the 1980s the Links had become run-down and demolition of the structure was considered, but the area and the bandstand were restored in 2009.

21

SEAFRONT BANDSTANDS

SEASIDE RESORTS were an eighteenth-century invention that expanded enormously during the Victorian period around the English and Welsh coasts. Their development paralleled that of the public parks, which were successors to the pleasure gardens of the Regency period.

By 1841 Brighton had forty thousand inhabitants, most of them permanent. But growth on the grand scale began with the railway age, as the railways enabled people to reach existing small settlements more cheaply and quickly. The main beneficiaries in the middle of the century were middle-class families. Over most of the country, working-class visitors relied on cheap excursions, organised by Sunday schools, employers, temperance societies or commercial promoters such as Thomas Cook. But by the last quarter of the nineteenth century many of the more accessible resorts had to cope with the novelty of a growing working-class presence with increased spending power, especially young people with wages. The growth of Clacton-on-Sea, Essex, was unprecedented: the census of 1881 showed a total population of 651; by 1901 it had reached 7,456. Its summer visitors also increased rapidly: in 1883 92,873 people paid to go on the pier; by 1893 this figure had rocketed to 327,451. Bandstands were a common and popular feature in Clacton-on-Sea.

In 1914 a new band pavilion was opened as part of the town's General Beautifying Programme. The bandstand was enclosed in a sunken pavilion with a glass front protecting the band and audience from the sea breezes. In 1936 the band pavilion was completely rebuilt and the bandstand was replaced by a stage, but it was still used for band concerts until the early 1970s.

The bandstand on East Parade, Bognor Regis, West Sussex, was built on the site of the grounds of the Royal Norfolk Hotel, which was sold in 1901 for £60. The Town Surveyor, Oswald Bridges, was then called upon to design a bandstand on the site for use by the large number of military bands that travelled around the resorts to entertain the public. By 1913 the venue was so popular that it was enlarged and deckchairs were made available for the comfort of the audience. The charge for these chairs helped to raise the £500 per year needed to hire the bands.

Opposite: Eastbourne Redoubt bandstand, East Sussex, built in 1935, with its unique semicircular design and blue domed roof, with main arena, middle and upper balconies and seats for 1,400. The bandstand formed part of the main seafront improvements, cost £28,000 to construct and was surmounted by a stainless steel spire. The first three concerts were given on 28 July 1935, attended by a total of 10,400 people, paying 3d each.

Clacton-on-Sea, Essex: the Walter MacFarlane bandstand was opened in 1899. Concerts by military bands were a regular feature during the Edwardian period. The town also had its own resident town band under conductor George Badger; the ten members of the band were paid £10 a week to share between them. The area round the bandstand was also a popular promenade area.

People have always been fascinated by the sea and have been continually drawn to coastal resorts. The special magnetism of the British seaside may have something to do with the remarkable structures made fashionable by the Victorians. Piers, promenades and bandstands were designed to be as individual in character as the particular resort where they were placed, but the primary function of most of them was to provide an area for 'promenading' or 'taking the air', taking shelter and admiring views. Bandstands were located near the sea, serving as viewing points for coastal scenery, as well as enabling bands to serenade holidaymakers. They were often located right on the seafront or on piers, promenades and in seaside gardens.

Clacton-on-Sea, Essex: the new 1914 band pavilion.

East Parade bandstand, Bognor Regis, West Sussex, was immensely popular in its day.

The Brighton Bandstand, also known as the Birdcage or the Bedford Square Bandstand, was designed by Phillip Causton Lockwood in 1883, manufactured by Walter MacFarlane & Company of the Saracen Foundry in Glasgow and constructed in 1884. The bandstand was designed as part of a project which included landscaped enclosures and covered shelters to improve facilities on the seafront in Brighton and Hove. It was originally intended as a sheltered area for ladies to rest in and to admire the sea views, but it was soon also sheltering bands and gentlemen. Philip Causton Lockwood had studied architecture in London before marrying a local woman and settling in Kemp Town, Brighton. He was the Borough Surveyor for over twenty-five years and designed several local structures, many incorporating the delicate latticed arches that are a significant feature of the bandstand. His seafront designs were expensive and controversial at the time but are now highly regarded.

Marine Parade bandstand, Eastbourne, East Sussex, in the 1920s, with glazing to protect musicians from the elements.

In the 1920s and 1930s there was a huge rise in the number of people able to take a holiday by the sea for a week or more. The unprecedented increase in the numbers of holidaymakers had far-reaching consequences for the appearance of the English coast. Firstly, the resorts had to be adapted and improved to cope with the larger numbers. Secondly, the inter-war years were the

Folkestone, Kent: The Leas bandstand, manufactured by the Elmbank foundry, erected in 1886 and now Grade II listed.

Phillip Causton Lockwood designed this bandstand at Brighton, manufactured by Walter MacFarlane's Saracen Foundry.

time when local councils began to assume the responsibility of running the seaside towns as a commercial enterprise.

In the Victorian and Edwardian eras it had been private enterprise that took the lead. In the inter-war years it was the local councillors who became directors of their towns. Seemingly ever-increasing sums of ratepayers' money were available to spend. Blackpool, not surprisingly, spent the most: £1,500,000 on a 7-mile promenade, £300,000 on indoor baths, £75,000 on an open-air pool and £250,000 on the entirely new Stanley Park. Brighton extended its promenade 6 miles to the new resort of Saltdean, added a new outdoor pool and revamped the aquarium. Bournemouth spent £250,000 on a new pavilion in 1929 and opened the Pier Approach Baths in 1937. Hastings spent £100,000 on the White Rock Pavilion, £180,000 on a new promenade and underground car park, and well over £150,000 on new swimming facilities. These figures might not seem huge by today's standards, but in those days a brand-new semi-detached house cost as little as £500.

With so much money to spend and local councils willing to spend it, many resorts were transformed in the 1920s and 1930s. At the beginning of the 1920s, seaside architecture followed the traditions of the Victorian age. The popular architectural style of the day was the classical or neo-Georgian, and this was well represented at the seaside and in the changing style and design of bandstands, which became much more grandiose.

The Worthing bandstand, West Sussex, an elegant 'birdcage' type, was built in 1897 west of the pier. For nearly thirty years holidaymakers and residents enjoyed numerous band concerts, with the Worthing Borough Band regularly performing there. In 1907 a shelter was erected between the bandstand and the beach to provide seating for promenaders to enjoy the music in comfort. In 1925 the bandstand was demolished and replaced with the Band Enclosure, designed by Adshead and Ramsey, which was later renamed the Lido. The original canopy over the stage was replaced in 1929 by the present domed roof. Over the years interest in band music declined and eventually, in 1957, the Lido was converted into an unheated swimming pool. It is now a family entertainment centre.

Worthing, West Sussex: the Band Enclosure, designed by Adshead and Ramsey, replaced the original 1897 bandstand as part of ongoing improvements to the resort.

By the 1930s there had been a dramatic shift in taste. The purpose was still the same – to create a fantasy world where the ordinary and dull would be banished – but the shape of that world had changed beyond recognition. No longer was the oriental pleasure palace the inspiration, but the sophistication of the south of France and the ocean liner. The idea was to bring buildings in the style of continental Europe to British shores, so that the middle and working classes could enjoy the atmosphere without the expense and the perceived dubious morals associated with the 'bright young things' of the smart set.

However, in the late 1950s and the 1960s, the long-established tradition of visiting the British coast was being challenged by the new possibilities of travelling abroad. With the subsequent decline of seaside resorts as well as parks, derelict and empty bandstands became symbolic of their fall from grace. The majority of coastal bandstands were ultimately removed.

Bexhill-on-Sea, East Sussex: Edwardian bandstand. There had been a demand for a new pavilion or 'winter garden' in Bexhill since about 1907. This was partly met by the development of Central Parade in 1910 and the opening of the Colonnade in 1911.

27

THE GREAT FOUNDRIES
OF THE 'IRON AGE'

THE PLACE of bandstands in park design and in the development of seaside towns cannot be considered without examining the huge impact of the great bandstand designers and foundries of the nineteenth and twentieth centuries, including the wonderful legacy left by three Scottish foundries, Walter MacFarlane's Saracen Foundry, the Lion Foundry of Kirkintilloch and George Smith's Sun Foundry.

The development of the bandstand in parks and on seaside promenades, particularly in relation to construction materials such as timber, iron and concrete, has been impressive. However, it is the more traditional octagonal bandstands – ornate, embellished and highly detailed structures composed primarily of cast iron – that are most associated with parks and seafronts. In some cases, iron bandstands have been replaced over the years with concrete, such as at Clifton Park, Rotherham, South Yorkshire, and coastal bandstands constructed of concrete have appeared as part of new developments, but the ornate, light and airy Victorian bandstand is most often a feature of our best-loved parks. To understand its significance to parks and promenades, it is essential to understand the use of iron in bandstand design and its effective employment by the great foundries of the time.

The introduction of iron as a constructional building material began in the eighteenth century, but in the nineteenth century its use became more widespread when adopted for more different purposes. Iron was *the* material of the nineteenth century and in the early part of the century it was seen as the wonder material of the day. This was before the structural potential of the material was understood fully, which did not happen until the later part of the century. In the eighteenth century the decorative potential of iron was adopted in traditional forms, such as in the construction of railings and gates, but towards the end of that century there were experiments in the substitution of iron for other materials, such as timber, which displayed the structural use of the material, even if its potential was not fully appreciated at the time.

Early-nineteenth-century landscape gardeners such as Humphry Repton and John Claudius Loudon were enthusiastic about the potential of iron.

Opposite:
Lincoln Arboretum. The Sun Foundry bandstand, with highly decorative baluster panels and spandrels, was sponsored by the Lincoln Lodges of Oddfellows and was installed in 1884 at a cost of £120. The names of the lodges are engraved on the solid blocks of Bramley Fallstone which form the base.

They praised its great strength in relation to its size when compared with other materials, such as wood or stone, used in buildings and other landscape features in their garden designs. Iron offered to garden designers and horticulturalists a strong, durable material that could be used for many different purposes, but which would not appear as large as objects made of more traditional materials. So structures, railings, gates and other objects of cast and wrought iron, because of their lightness of form, offered a more sympathetic relationship with the natural world of the garden.

The decorative advantages of iron were also an important factor in its widespread adoption in gardens during the nineteenth century. Both wrought and cast iron presented advantages over other materials. Wrought iron could be worked into different shapes while hot, and through repeated heating and beating or rolling could take on shapes that could be used for constructional or decorative purposes. A great discovery of the early nineteenth century was the recognition of the potential of wrought iron for constructional purposes, but the potential of cast iron was also more widely understood during the century. Cast iron was very important for decorative purposes, being able to adopt the form and relief surface of the moulded shape into which the molten cast iron was poured, and so offered the possibility of replication and repetition with little need for craftsmanship beyond the making of the initial pattern. This was in contrast to wrought iron, each member of which would have to be worked by hand, first having been heated to a temperature where it was malleable and could be worked by beating and other processes, to bend, twist and cut the material to the desired shape. The characteristics of the two different materials can be very clearly seen in the ways in which they were used.

Cast iron poured in a Falkirk foundry for the replacement of the Albert Park bandstand, Middlesbrough, which was made in 2005.

The different uses of iron as a decorative and structural material in public parks were many and included applications to bandstands, pavilions, shelters, bridges, seats and benches, light standards or pillars, ornamental vases, fountains, drinking fountains and other sculptural purposes.

Like conservatories and winter gardens, bandstands were often made of iron. In many instances cast iron was used, but wrought iron was also employed, particularly for light lattice rafters to support roofs. Cast-iron columns were a common feature of bandstand design. Frequently these

An extract from a MacFarlane's catalogue which depicts a composite sketch of castings for a pier. The picture includes gates, a shelter, a fountain, lamp standards and a bandstand.

The anatomy of a Lion Foundry No. 40 bandstand:
A – Gate
B – Newel post
C – Radial spandrel
D – Centre cresting
E – Corner terminal
F – Centre spandrel
G – Dome
H – Terminal
I – Dome top ring cresting
J – Dome bottom ring
K – Main roof
L – Column
M – Baluster panel.

Design detail of the bandstand in Hyde Corporation Public Park, near Manchester, a Lion Foundry no. 23 design. Officially opened on 18 May 1922, it is now a Grade II listed building. The bandstand was originally surrounded by movable glass partitions and during the 1930s the bandstand hosted two concerts every Sunday.

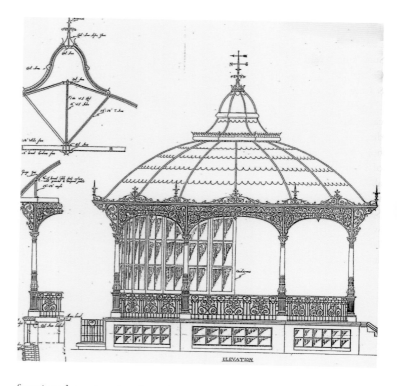

functioned as rainwater downpipes, so it is not unusual to find that these pipes are sometimes split from the action of freezing water inside. Decorative castings around the eaves, cresting along the top of the gutter or the ridge, and a finial or weathervane at the centre of the roof were common elements, but these are now usually missing, at least in part, and it is rare to see a bandstand with all its ironwork intact. Bandstands were usually elevated on a platform for visibility, and the decorative iron stairs, handrail and railings around the perimeter are often broken or missing because they are vulnerable to vandalism. The underside of the bandstand roof was frequently boarded to serve as a sounding board, like the tester above a pulpit, and the base upon which the bandstand was raised was sometimes a masonry construction.

With the rise in popularity of the bandstand, the swathe of public parks being created across the country and advancements in production techniques, a number of designers and foundries came to dominate the market. These foundries had a major role to play. Foundries producing bandstands in the nineteenth and early twentieth centuries included Walter MacFarlane's Saracen Foundry in Glasgow, George Smith's Sun Foundry in Glasgow and the Lion Foundry at Kirkintilloch, East Dunbartonshire. Smaller foundries that produced fewer bandstands included James Allan Senior & Sons' Elmbank Foundry of Glasgow, Hill & Smith Ltd of Brierley Hill, Hill & Sons' Sun Foundry of Alloa, J. & A. Law of Glasgow, McDowall Steven & Company's Milton Iron Works of London and Glasgow and Yates Haywood & Company of Rotherham, South Yorkshire.

A small number of Scottish foundries were the most prolific in making cast-iron products, and in particular bandstands. This was partly due to the discovery of black-band ironstone in 1802, followed by the invention of the hot blast process in 1828 by James Beaumont Neilson, enabling vast reserves of iron ore to be processed cheaply and in a viable manner with pit coal. The abundant supply of coal and ore in Scotland, coupled with the suitability of the pig iron for ornamental work, prompted the industry to develop in Scotland, in particular on the west coast. For a considerable time, Scotland was an exceptional producer and manufacturer of architectural cast ironwork, and the Saracen Foundry of Walter MacFarlane & Company Ltd in Glasgow was a major exponent of the industry.

> In this new foundry an immense variety of work is turned out, and art in cast iron is cultivated to such an extent, and with such an amount of success as are not known elsewhere, either in this country or abroad ... MacFarlane's castings are favourably known in every civilised nation in the world...
>
> [*Notices of Some of the Principal Manufactures of the West Coast of Scotland*, Glasgow, 1876]

Below: A cast-iron bandstand during construction; it is a Lion Foundry no. 23 model.

Walter MacFarlane & Company Ltd was one of a small number of Scottish architectural ironfounders who came to prominence in the nineteenth century. Despite being considered late starters in comparison to others, they soon came to dominate this industry, quickly matching and eventually surpassing their rivals to become the most prolific architectural ironfounders in Britain. Their execution of design and marketing of products, through catalogues of considerable artistic achievement, were vital. The principle of prefabrication in particular was clearly demonstrable through these catalogues, and no doubt a major factor in their success. The catalogues allowed customers to choose elements that they preferred and often enabled individual designs to be created. Many customers, however, preferred to choose a complete design based on existing patterns and models. This, and the seemingly unrelenting ability for self-promotion by the owners, made for a seductive operation.

At the same time, the distribution of their products throughout the world was astounding. Even now, when much architectural ironwork has been removed from the landscape, it is still possible to find the distinctive diamond trademark of the company on many bandstands.

Walter MacFarlane developed his company in such a way that he outstretched the competition, putting established companies such as George Smith's Sun Foundry into the shade and eventually out of business. Known as a shrewd businessman, his perceived arrogance was demonstrated by the putting of his name on every piece of iron to leave the foundry. His prolific publications surely helped to perpetuate the aura that Saracen Foundry developed and maintains even to this day.

Between 1849 and 1850 Walter MacFarlane went into partnership with Thomas Russell, his brother-in-law, and his friend James Marshall, a Glasgow businessman. In 1851 the company took over a disused brass foundry in Saracen Lane in the Gallowgate, naming the foundry after the street. The company thrived in Saracen Lane and by 1861 it employed 120 people. The company outgrew the premises and, looking to expand, relocated to Washington Street in 1862. However, the overwhelming success of the company continued and a decision was made to move again to what became the third and final Saracen Foundry, at Possilpark, built and expanded to a vast scale in 1872. The third Saracen foundry eventually covered 80 acres.

Sir William Stirling Maxwell visited the site on 11 November 1875 and wrote in his diary:

I was struck with the immense growth of Glasgow on its North side … we stopped at Walter MacFarlane's Saracen Foundry newly built on the Possil Estate of which he feud 100 acres – a speculation likely

A bandstand from an incredibly detailed MacFarlane catalogue, a feature of this successful and growing business.

to make a great return. The establishment employs from 70–80 Clerks, and almost 1,400 workmen, and the workshops extend over 8 acres, all under cover. It is a very interesting and picturesque site. Home by the 4.20 p.m. train.

Whilst Walter MacFarlane remained the figurehead of the company, his partners Thomas Russell and James Marshall became intimately involved in the development and running of the business. Each became a wealthy man in his own right. In the 1870s Thomas Russell donated a bandstand to his adopted town of Rothesay.

By the 1890s the Saracen Foundry was a major employer, providing work for around 1,200 people, and now led by Walter MacFarlane Junior, under whose leadership it reached its peak. After 1918 the firm moved on to the production of enamelled baths for the domestic market and rainwater goods for building façades, which became a significant percentage of output. The Second World War practically ended the production of ornamental work, with most of the foundry contributing to the war effort and doing only limited engineering work. As a result of drastic changes in the market, the foundry at Possilpark eventually closed in 1967.

Ropner Park bandstand, Stockton-on-Tees, opened in 1893, is a restored Walter MacFarlane model no. 279 bandstand.

Borough Gardens, Dorchester, Dorset. The Walter MacFarlane bandstand was presented by a former MP, Colonel W. E. Bryner, in July 1898, to celebrate Queen Victoria's Diamond Jubilee. Concerts would start at 8 p.m. on Sundays, after the Boys Brigade and congregation had come out of chapel. 'An accordion band and a man playing a saw all made deep impressions on local people.'

Saracen Foundry bandstands are still the most frequently found in parks today, with significant structures surviving in many public parks, from Penzance in Cornwall (Morrab Gardens), via the Isle of Wight (Ventnor Park) and Wolverhampton (East Park) to Liverpool (Stanley Park), and north to

Abbey Gardens, Hexham, Northumberland: a Walter MacFarlane no. 249 model with its intricate and detailed cresting, erected in 1912.

Harehill Park, Littleborough, Greater Manchester: the Walter MacFarlane bandstand with its overhanging eaves and decorative frill was presented by Mr J. Cryer in 1902, a year after the park was opened.

Dunfermline and St Andrews in Fife and Forfar in Angus. MacFarlane was known for diversity of design and workmanship, yet it is often quite easy to recognise a MacFarlane bandstand as two models were especially popular, the 249 and 279, the latter often 'topped by open scrolled ironwork in the

Victoria Park, Macclesfield, Cheshire: the bandstand erected in 1894, from the Walter MacFarlane Saracen Foundry, with its distinctive 'onion dome'.

Exhibition Park, Newcastle upon Tyne. The bandstand is the only surviving structure from the Jubilee Exhibition of 1887, manufactured by Walter MacFarlane's Saracen Foundry. It is an unusual example of a MacFarlane design, not found anywhere else.

Stanley Park, Liverpool. The original design of the park (1866) was by Edward Kemp, a pioneer of public park design. The Walter MacFarlane model 279 bandstand was added in 1890 as part of a later phase.

shape of an onion dome'. There are at least twenty remaining 279 models in Britain, showing how popular they were. The example at Horsham, West Sussex, is described in its English Heritage Listing thus:

> Octagonal. Raised on a painted stone plinth with rectangular moulded panels on each face. Low pyramidal lead roof in eight triangular sections, topped by open scrolled ironwork in the shape of an onion dome. Spike on top. Overhanging eaves with decorative frill and scrolled ironwork cresting above facing north, south, east and west. Eight cast-iron columns with Ionic capitals, annulets and octagonal bases. These carry an octagonal frame of horizontal girders under the eaves. In the angles are brackets of decorative ironwork with lyre motif. Open ironwork balustrades with central floriated panels. Ironwork stair with plain handrail and two twisted baluster shafts.

George Smith & Company Ltd was founded in 1858 and was very much contemporary with and therefore a business rival to Walter MacFarlane & Company. Founded by George Smith at 64 Port Dundas Road in Glasgow, the company quickly expanded, moving in 1875 to Parliamentary Road, where

Ventnor, Isle of Wight. The bandstand was originally erected on the pier in 1887 and moved to Ventnor Park in 1903. It is an unusual assembly of MacFarlane components, as illustrated in the sixth edition catalogue of c. 1882.

The bandstand at Albert Park, Middlesbrough, replaced as part of the town's principal park. An unusual design not seen anywhere else in the country, the castings are very intricate.

West Park, Wolverhampton: 'a most generous gift was that of Charles Pelham Villiers, MP for Wolverhampton, who was unable to attend the grand opening of the park, but, instead, gave a beautiful cast iron bandstand.' *The Builder*, in 1882, reported that the McDowall Steven bandstand 'was inaugurated with considerable demonstrations on Whit-Monday'. It was 'greatly enlarged' some time before 1901.

they remained to 1896. By the 1870s and 1880s they were able competitors and equal in size to the Saracen Foundry, although Walter MacFarlane would eventually outstrip them in terms of production and sales. The Sun Foundry, despite being less prolific than the Saracen Foundry, is, however, considered by many to be superior in terms of style, design and quality, and this can be seen from the bandstands that remain in parks, as well as from the few images that still exist. They are extremely detailed, with complex baluster panels, spandrels and cresting. The Glasgow Sun Foundry produced a range of excellent designs for several bandstands that still remain. These include Clapham Common in London, Lincoln Arboretum, Leazes Park in Newcastle upon Tyne, Albert Park in Middlesbrough, Mesnes Park in Wigan and The Links in Nairn.

In 1896 the Sun Foundry relocated, indicating that the company was starting to struggle with the continued rise of the nearby Saracen Foundry. Only three years later, it had closed. The Sun Foundry did not appear to embrace the constructional opportunities of cast iron for building that both the Saracen Foundry and the Lion Foundry took. George Smith had relocated to Alloa and established the Sun Foundry, Alloa, just before the main company went out of business in 1899. The Alloa works became a significant foundry in its own right.

McDowall Steven & Company Ltd also had its roots among the pioneers of the cast-iron industry in Scotland and played an important role in designing

and manufacturing bandstands. The Phoenix Foundry in Glasgow, the first true ornamental iron foundry in the city, was started in 1804 by Thomas Edington, whose experience and wealth arose from his involvement with the Carron, Cramond, Muirkirk and Clyde ironworks. His son James worked with him at the Phoenix Foundry before departing to establish the Eagle Foundry with John McDowall around 1820. In 1828, following changes to the partnership, they became McDowall & Robertson & Milton Foundry at Port Dundas, later becoming McDowall & Company Ltd in Port Dundas from 1844 to 1861. The most prolific period of the foundry's success followed another move, in 1862, to 142 Woodside Road in Glasgow, where the company became McDowall Steven & Company Ltd and the foundry Milton Ironworks.

Several excellent bandstands of theirs are still found in a number of parks. These show innovation in construction, using wrought-iron sheet with cast-iron roof formers, unlike the predominantly timber construction of most Saracen examples. The quality of the bandstands in constructional detail is matched by the fine detail and quality of their castings. Many of their bandstands were also unique in style and design and they were the only manufacturer who used double circles of columns, as seen in Wolverhampton's West Park and The Quarry, Shrewsbury. It is thought that they closed in 1909. The firm was resurrected in 1916 at the Laurieston Iron Works in Falkirk, until 1930, when it became the Allied Iron Founders Ltd of Falkirk.

Other remaining bandstands include Valentines Park, Ilford; North Lodge Park, Darlington; Roker Park, Sunderland; and Duthie Park, Aberdeen.

In 1880 three staff from the Saracen Foundry left the company and set up the Lion Foundry in Kirkintilloch near Glasgow. James Brown had been a clerk in the order department, James Jackson a salesman and Robert Hudson

Below Left:
The Quarry, Shrewsbury, Shropshire. The bandstand is described in its listing as 'cast iron ... octagonal (with) ogee roof surmounted with a weather vane. Eight plain outer pillars and eight inner barley sugar pillars with wrought iron railings and steps.'

Below right:
Roker Park, Sunderland: an excellent McDowall Steven bandstand, erected in 1880.

Handsworth Park bandstand in Birmingham was erected in 1903 by the Lion Foundry, with Art Nouveau-inspired baluster panels and spandrels.

Hyde Park, Hyde, Greater Manchester: the Lion Foundry bandstand was officially opened on 18 May 1922.

a fitter at Saracen. The following year William Cassells, who had been a designer and draughtsman at Saracen, left to take up the same post at Lion. The design references are apparent in the work of the Lion Foundry from the point Cassells joined. He was succeeded by James Leitch, who was responsible for many of the Art Nouveau designs produced by the company. Originally

known as Jackson, Brown, Hudson & Cuthbert, the company changed its name to the Lion Foundry in 1885. In 1893 the company became a limited liability company with the formation of the Lion Foundry Company Ltd. The name is still registered, although it has been dormant for many years.

Like its competitors and local contemporaries, Lion Foundry produced ornamental cast ironwork, including railings, crestings and terminals in its early days, but it quickly started to manufacture fountains, bandstands, canopies and larger structures. Like its contemporaries, it produced pattern books, which grew larger as the company developed. Significantly, the Lion Foundry outlasted Walter MacFarlane & Company by twenty years, surviving in Kirkintilloch until closure in 1984.

Its bandstands included the North Embankment, Dartmouth; Victoria Park, Newbury; Handsworth Park, Birmingham; Locke Park, Barnsley; Hyde Park, Hyde; Victoria Park, Southport; Carmarthen Park, Carmarthen; Peel Park, Kirkintilloch; and Lewisvale Park, Musselburgh.

Of the English foundries that produced bandstands, the one that had the most impact was Hill & Smith of Brierley Hill, West Midlands. It manufactured bandstands for many parks. Those which remain include Hayes Town Hall Park, Hayes, Middlesex; Abington Park, Northampton; Mary Stevens Park, Stourbridge; Victoria Park, Ilkeston; Queen's Park, Loughborough; Saltwell Park, Gateshead; Horden Welfare Park, Horden, County Durham; Congleton Park, Congleton; Victoria Park, Denton, near Manchester; Sefton Park, Liverpool; Aberdare Public Park, Aberdare; and Bedwellty Park, Tredegar.

Despite the decline of the great foundries, which followed the neglect of parks and seaside resorts and the consequent loss of bandstands, a small number of conservation specialists have arisen and are at the centre of the revival of many of Britain's parks. These specialists have recreated many of the skills of the old foundries and have researched many Victorian designs in detail. Much of the Lion Foundry archives remains, having been saved by the local librarian, though regrettably much of the MacFarlane legacy was lost. What remains is valuable and is now used by the conservation specialists and local authorities in restoring and recreating many of the bandstands lost or sadly neglected for the latter part of the twentieth century.

Horden Welfare Park, County Durham, was created in the 1920s. The Hill & Smith bandstand dates from 1928. The quality of their wrought ironwork was very durable. They used cast iron for the columns, while brackets, railings and ornamental friezes were wrought. Designs were much more simplistic than a George Smith or Walter MacFarlane design.

DECLINE AND REVIVAL

FROM THE 1950s the deterioration of parks and bandstands was considerable and many of the latter were removed. Those which did survive and were reasonably well maintained during the 1960s, 1970s and early 1980s also began to suffer as cuts in parks services became acute, and in many cases bandstands were simply boarded up.

It was after the Second World War that the influence of the parks movement started to decline. The influence of modernism in planning and architecture spread to the design of parks, where decoration disappeared and green deserts appeared that were easier to maintain; playing fields dominated and sporting activity became more popular than passive recreation. An exception was the garden city movement, one of the main principles of which was that adequate provision of parks and open spaces should be included. The grandiose architectural display Olmsted was so wary of had long since disappeared.

The decline of urban parks did not become truly felt until the 1970s. With the removal of railings and gates in the 1940s, ostensibly to provide metal for the war effort (more likely it was dumped in the Atlantic Ocean), parks had became open to abuse. Local government reorganisation saw parks departments disappear, absorbed into 'leisure services departments', where they competed for budgets with new indoor leisure centres. Parks lost their identity and their role, and, as they created little revenue for local authorities, budgets were easily cut, maintenance reduced and features that were falling into disrepair and being vandalised were removed. These included statues, glasshouses, water features and, sadly, many bandstands. The individual character of each park comes from its location, design and landscaping, and from the planting, buildings, statues and memorials within. By the mid-1990s the impact of these detrimental factors on the fabric of parks had become increasingly evident.

In 2001 the Urban Parks Forum carried out a major survey of local authority-owned parks, focusing on parks of historic interest. The Public Park Assessment found that 'the loss of many of the features traditionally associated with parks and gardens is extensive and acute. Particularly badly

Opposite:
The Meadows,
Edinburgh: the
Lion Foundry
bandstand had
become
delapidated by
the 1950s.

Above and above right: The impressive McDowall Steven bandstand in North Lodge Park, Darlington, as erected in 1903, and seen boarded up in 2010, having lost all its baluster panels, finials and crests. It was restored in the summer of 2010.

Right: The Meadows, Edinburgh: the bandstand being removed and scrapped in 1953.

Nuns Moor Park, Newcastle upon Tyne: only the masonry base marks the site of the bandstand.

affected, with losses of between 50 per cent and 71 per cent are Ice Houses, Public Glass Houses, Bandstands, Paddling Pools and Fountains'.

An extract from a local authority report in 1995 stated:

> Park buildings are a maintenance liability and can attract vandalism. They can also be visually intrusive and will be reduced to a minimum needed, consistent with the effective management of the parks. Where listed buildings exist they will, if possible, be found a long term use. Other buildings will be progressively eliminated.

By the end of the twentieth century few historic parks could be classed as being in good condition; many bandstands had been lost and those that remained were in extremely poor condition. Cities such as Bradford, Leeds, Manchester, Glasgow, Newcastle upon Tyne and Sheffield had bandstands in

A Walter MacFarlane bandstand in North Park, Darlington, Co. Durham, abused and neglected.

Saughton Park, Edinburgh: the Lion Foundry bandstand being demolished in 1987. It is shown below in its prime, with the band of the Gordon Highlanders playing.

most of their parks in their heyday at the start of the twentieth century, but most of these have long since been removed. Saughton Park in Edinburgh was the site in 1908 of the Scottish National Exhibition, where one of the exhibits was a bandstand. When the exhibition closed, the bandstand was removed to Marine Gardens, Portobello, near Edinburgh. In spite of its

relocation, another bandstand was erected at one of the entrances to Saughton Park in 1909, along with an identical bandstand in the Meadows. The latter lasted less than fifty years and was dismantled and scrapped in 1953. The Saughton Park bandstand lasted longer but was dismantled and removed in 1987. It was still in storage in 2010 awaiting a new lease of life somewhere in an Edinburgh park.

Myrtle Park bandstand in Bingley, West Yorkshire, erected in 1913, is in poor condition in 2010 and seems neglected and forlorn in comparison with the rest of the park, which is well maintained. The original baluster panels have long since been removed and replaced with inappropriate and unsympathetic highway-style pedestrian barriers.

Locke Park bandstand in Barnsley was erected in 1908 and has lost its original baluster panels, crestings and corner terminals, as well as the original roof covering. Although in reasonable condition, it has retained little of its past splendour.

West Park bandstand in Long Eaton, Derbyshire, which was donated by the Co-operative Society in 1935, is in poor condition in 2010, despite its popularity, having lost all its original baluster panels.

Myrtle Park, Bingley, West Yorkshire: the bandstand was manufactured by Walter MacFarlane in 1913.

Edwardian ladies in the Lion Foundry bandstand in Locke Park, Barnsley, South Yorkshire.

Regular use of Clapham Common bandstand in south London continued until well after the Second World War, it being used by bands such as Dire Straits and the Darts in 1977, but it gradually fell out of use. By the end of the twentieth century, it was in a severe state of decay, with the roof pigeon-infested, the ceiling boards rotten, cracks in rusted columns, the tarmac surrounds and drains uneven and broken. In 1977 English Heritage had put the bandstand on their 'Buildings at Risk' register, but its full restoration was completed in 2009.

The Locke Park, Barnsley, bandstand being prepared for the annual Beer and Blues Festival. It is still a popular venue in the park, but its condition is deteriorating.

However, the future for many historic parks and their bandstands became much brighter in the late 1990s, with the most significant investment of funding seen since Victorian times, brought about by the National Lottery and the Heritage Lottery Fund. More than eighty bandstands have been either fully restored or replaced. Between 1979 and 2001, more than half the 438 bandstands in historic parks had been demolished, were unused or vandalised as parks departments continued to cut their maintenance budgets. But between 1996 and 2010, reinvestment in parks was substantial, amounting to over £500 million, which included work on many bandstand projects.

Modern construction firms rediscovered the old drawings, catalogues and manuscripts of the Saracen, Lion and Sun foundries and others and used these as templates for the restoration of neglected bandstands. Lost Art from Wigan identified the maker of the South Shields bandstand as the MacFarlane foundry in Glasgow, whose few remaining catalogues are in the library at Kirkintilloch.

Clapham Common, London: the George Smith Sun Foundry bandstand, derelict at the end of the twentieth century,

The same bandstand in 2009, fully restored after a campaign by the Friends of Clapham Common.

After checking the catalogues and taking photographs of the illustrations, they were able to get wood-carvers to pick out the details and have since created castings from the carvings, including as much detail as possible, in order to be faithful to the original design.

Broadfield Park in Rochdale was the town's first public park, dating back to the 1870s and commanding splendid views of the town centre's civic quarter, including the Grade I listed town hall, which is set against the backdrop of the Pennines. The original bandstand was erected in 1893, supplied by Walter MacFarlane's Saracen Foundry, and was fully restored in 2005 to the exact original specifications. It received a Civic Society Award in 2005.

This time, the foundry responsible for the restoration used large quantities of recycled aluminium in the fine castings rather than the cast iron of the original product. The bandstand is now the venue for regular concerts and events in the park.

The Albert Park bandstand in Middlesbrough was erected in the summer of 1871 by George Smith & Company and an 1871 newspaper article described it thus: 'a beautiful octagonal iron stand for the band is approaching completion and is an ornament to the centre of the park, the light columns

South Marine Park, South Shields, Tyne and Wear: the re-created bandstand, based on the 1904 original model by Walter MacFarlane & Company.

Broadfield Park, Rochdale: the bandstand seen in an old postcard, and in 2009, fully restored to MacFarlane's exacting standards.

and elegant roof giving the structure quite an oriental aspect.' After considerable research, based on postcards, old photographs and Sun Foundry archives, the bandstand was refabricated in a Scottish foundry, and replaced in 2005.

Albert Park, Middlesbrough: the original bandstand, and the bandstand that replaced it in 2005, made to the original Sun Foundry design.

Palfrey Park in Walsall was officially opened to the public on 29 May 1886, at a cost of £90. Unfortunately, the original George Smith bandstand was removed from the park in 1948, its demise attributed to the decline in interest in summer concerts. A new replacement bandstand was completed in 2006 at a cost of £200,000. No original designs or plan for the bandstand survived, and only two historic photographs were available. Brick samples were taken from the park lodge, which was built around the same time, to guide the choice of brick.

The bandstand in Weston Park, Sheffield, is the only surviving Victorian bandstand in a Sheffield park, which is remarkable considering that they were

such features in most of the city's parks, including the Botanical Gardens, Hillsborough Park and Endcliffe Park. It was designed in 1874 by the Sheffield architects Flockton and Gibbs but was not built until about 1900, paid for by the profits of the electric tramways. It was fabricated by James Allan & Sons of Glasgow at the Elmbank Foundry as one of a pair commissioned for Sheffield parks (the other was in Hillsborough Park). Its most interesting and unusual feature is the retractable sash windows, which drop down below the floor. This unique

Left and below:
Palfrey Park,
Walsall: the
original bandstand,
and its modern
replacement
following the Sun
Foundry's original
design.

Weston Park,
Sheffield: an
excellent Elmbank
Foundry
bandstand.

feature, as well as sheltering the musicians, also helped to project the sound from their instruments. The bandstand was in regular use until the mid-1970s and was restored in 2008.

Clifton Park in Rotherham, South Yorkshire, was opened in 1891. The original bandstand was, however, removed to Masbrough Recreation Ground. A new concrete bandstand was erected on the site of the old bandstand and was opened in May 1928. It remains to the present day but is an excellent example of how designs have evolved. It was renovated, and reopened by Queen Elizabeth II in May 1991, and restored further in 2009.

The structure in Victoria Park, Denton, near Manchester, was first designed and built by Hill & Smith in their Brierley Hill Foundry. Their 1904 catalogue described it as having an octagonal plinth, and wrought- and cast-iron

balustrades attached to cast-iron pillars supporting a domed roof with an ornamental weathervane; it would be supplied and erected for the sum of £172 10s 0d. The bandstand was restored in 2007.

Clifton Park, Rotherham, South Yorkshire: the original Victorian bandstand, and the 1928 bandstand, restored in 2009.

The light and airy structures that the Victorians designed were often architecturally wonderful and ranged in design from simplistic to magnificently ornate, but what they really were, and are once again, is the centre and heart of a park. The bandstand and its surrounding area, where people stand and listen, watch, gaze and admire, is the focal point of a park. But a bandstand is, however, merely an empty shell unless music is played on it, and increasingly local authorities and other organisations are realising this again.

Derelict bandstands were once symbolic of the decline of a park. Now restored bandstands are representative of the renewal of many popular parks and are central to many park

regeneration initiatives, again owned and enjoyed by their local communities. In other words, the restoration of a bandstand shows that a community cares. For instance, in 2010 'Bandstand Busking' is now a regular monthly event that gives up-and-coming musicians the opportunity to perform in the underused bandstands dotted around London's parks, and the annual Bandstand Marathon aims to raise the profile of bandstands by simultaneous concerts arranged on a single weekend every year.

At the beginning of the twentieth century nearly every seaside resort had a number of bandstands but now, sadly, images on old seaside postcards are the only reminder of their existence. Unlike Britain's many urban parks, there has not been a renaissance on the coast but there have been a number of significant restorations.

The Brighton Birdcage Bandstand was considered one of the finest examples of a Victorian bandstand at a seaside resort and is now the only one remaining in Brighton, where in 1910 there were eight bandstands, including one further along the seafront in Hove, where the Babylon Lounge now stands. That bandstand was torn down in 1965.

Victoria Park, Denton, Greater Manchester: the reopening of the Hill & Smith bandstand in 2007.

The Brighton bandstand continued to be a popular venue for bands throughout the early 1960s but thereafter it began to decay from neglect, and the bridge connecting it to King's Road was removed in the 1970s for reasons of safety. The bandstand was left unused and it is likely that forty years of neglect would have seen its demise if the Brighton Bandstand Campaign had not been set up in 2007.

Brighton: the restored Walter MacFarlane Birdcage Bandstand.

In May 2007 Brighton and Hove City Council, with the backing of all political parties, agreed to fund its renovation. The restoration work started in September 2008, and the roof and cast-iron metal superstructure were restored in two different Sussex specialist workshops. The 2,500 people who signed the petition can now see it fully restored and in use as both a musical venue and a café.

From a vantage point behind a music stand on the bandstand, the obvious pleasure that people would take in stopping to listen on a sunny Sunday afternoon must have been hugely rewarding. Bandstands are the least cynical of public spaces, free and with no motive other than to make a sunny afternoon a little more pleasant. After a period of criminal neglect, they are starting to be loved again and a new era of public music is under way. All things considered, the Victorians probably had it right.

FURTHER READING

Clapham Society and Friends of Clapham Common. *The Clapham Bandstand, the Story of the Restoration*. Clapham Common Bandstand Restoration Fund, 2007.

Conway, Hazel. *Public Parks*. Shire, 1996.

Downing, Andrew Jackson. *A Treatise on the Theory and Practice of Landscape Gardening*. Funk & Wagnalls, 1967.

Harper Smith, A. and T. *Acton Park, a Short History*. Acton Past and Present Series no. 48, 2001.

Scottish Ironwork Foundation. *MacFarlane's Architectural Ironwork*. Harlaw Heritage, 2006.

Starr, S. Frederick. *The Oberlin Book of Bandstands*. The Preservation Press, 1987.

Woudstra, Jan, and Fieldhouse, Ken. *The Regeneration of Public Parks*. E. & F. N. Spon, 2000.

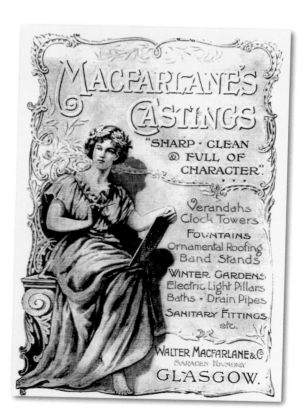

The range of features available in many of the MacFarlane catalogues.

GAZETTEER

The following bandstands are worth visiting:

Berkshire
Newbury: Victoria Park. Reading: Forbury Gardens.

Cambridgeshire
Wisbech: The Park.

Cheshire
Chester: The Groves. Congleton: Congleton Park. Crewe: Queen's Park. Macclesfield: Victoria Park. Widnes: Victoria Park.

Cornwall
Falmouth: Gyllyndune Gardens. Penzance: Morrab Gardens.

Cumbria
Grange-over-Sands: The Park. Penrith: Castle Park.

Derbyshire
Belper: River Gardens. Chesterfield: Queen's Park. Ilkeston: Victoria Park. Matlock: Hall Leys Gardens.

Devon
Dartmouth: North Embankment.

Dorset
Dorchester: Borough Gardens.

Durham, County
Consett: Blackhill and Consett Park. Darlington: North Lodge Park. Hartlepool: Ward Jackson Park. Horden: Horden Welfare Park.

Essex
Colchester: Upper Castle Park.

Gloucestershire and Bristol
Bristol: Castle Park. Cheltenham: Montpellier Gardens.

Hampshire
Basingstoke: War Memorial Park. Eastleigh: The Park. Romsey: War Memorial Park.

Isle of Wight
Ventnor: Ventnor Park.

Kent
Canterbury: Dane John Gardens. Sevenoaks: The Vine.

Leicestershire
Loughborough: Queen's Park.

Lincolnshire
Lincoln: Arboretum.

London, Greater
Battersea: Battersea Park, SW11. Bow: Victoria Park, E9. Camberwell: Myatt's Fields Park, SE5. Clapham: Clapham Common, SW4. Forest

Hill: Horniman Gardens, SE23. Golders Green: Golders Hill Park, NW11. Greenwich: Greenwich Park, SE10. Hayes (Middlesex): Town Hall Park. Ilford: Valentines Park. Leyton: Coronation Gardens, E10. Merton: John Innes Park, SW20. Queen's Park: Queen's Park, NW6. Rotherhithe: Southwark Park, SE16. Stoke Newington: Clissold Park, N16. Sydenham: Crystal Palace Park, SE9. Uxbridge: Fassnidge Park. West Ham: West Ham Park, E15. Westminster: Hyde Park, W2; Kensington Gardens, W2; Regent's Park, NW1.

Manchester, Greater

Denton: Victoria Park. Hyde: Hyde Park. Littleborough: Harehill Park. Rochdale: Broadfield Park. Stockport: Vernon Park. Wigan: Mesnes Park.

Merseyside

Birkenhead: Birkenhead Park. Bootle: Derby Park. Liverpool: Sefton Park; Stanley Park. Southport: Lord Street; Victoria Park.

Norfolk

King's Lynn: The Walks. Norwich: Chapelfield Gardens; Waterloo Park.

Northamptonshire

Kettering: Rockingham Road Park. Northampton: Abington Park.

Northumberland

Blyth: Beach. Hexham: Abbey Gardens.

Oxfordshire

Bicester: Garth Park.

Shropshire

Shrewsbury: The Quarry. Telford: Town Park.

Somerset

Clevedon: seafront. Weston-super-Mare: Grove Park.

Staffordshire

Stoke-on-Trent: Hanley Park.

Sussex, East

Bexhill-on-Sea: De La Warr Pavilion. Brighton: King's Road Promenade. Hastings: Alexandra Park.

Sussex, West

Horsham: Carfax.

Tyne and Wear

Gateshead: Saltwell Park. Newcastle upon Tyne: Leazes Park. South Shields: South Marine Park. Sunderland: Barnes Park; Mowbray Gardens; Roker Park.

An advertisement for Walter MacFarlane's Saracen Foundry.

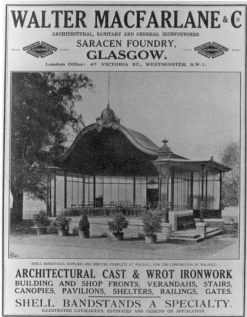

Warwickshire

Leamington Spa: Pump Room Gardens. Rugby: Caldecott Park.

West Midlands

Birmingham: Botanical Gardens; Handsworth Park; Lightwoods Park.
Stourbridge: Mary Stevens Park. Walsall: Arboretum; Palfrey Park.
Wolverhampton: East Park; West Park.

Wiltshire

Swindon: Old Town Gardens.

Worcestershire

Great Malvern: Priory Park. Worcester: Gheluvelt Park.

Yorkshire, North

Middlesbrough: Albert Park.

Yorkshire, South

Elsecar: Elsecar Park. Rotherham: Clifton Park. Sheffield: Weston Park.

Yorkshire, West

Halifax: People's Park. Huddersfield: Greenhead Park.

Wales

Aberdare: Aberdare Public Park. Abergavenny, Bailey Park. Cardiff:
Grange Gardens; Victoria Park. Carmarthen: Carmarthen Park.
Merthyr Tydfil: Cyfarthfa Park. Neath: Victoria Gardens. Pontypridd:
Memorial Park.
Tredegar: Bedwellty
Park.

Scotland

Aberdeen: Duthie
Park. Brechin: Public
Park. Crieff: MacRosty
Park. Dumfries: Dock
Park. Dunfermline:
Public Park;
Pittencrieff Park.
Forfar: Reid Park.
Glasgow: Kelvingrove
Park; Queen's Park.
Hamilton: Public Park.
Kirkintilloch: Peel
Park. Musselburgh:
Lewisvale Park. Nairn:
The Links. St Andrews:
The Scores.

Opening of
North Lodge Park,
Darlington,
19 September
2010. After tireless
campaigning by the
local Friends
Group, this
stunning McDowall
Steven bandstand
is now central to
the life of the park
once again, having
been carefully
restored by Lost
Art from Wigan

INDEX